bathe in it or

sleep

poems by

Kim Triedman

Winner of the 2008 Main Street Rag Chapbook Contest

MAIN STREET RAG PUBLISHING COMPANY
CHARLOTTE, NORTH CAROLINA

Cover image: "Beauty," oil on canvas, Monjushri Micah Schatz
Author photo by: Julie Triedman

Grateful acknowledgment is made to the publications in which most of
these poems first appeared, sometimes in different form:

The Aurorean: "Think of it this way"
Poet's Ink: "Physical memory," "Residue"
The New Writer: "Chaos theory," "Fractured," "Distance"
Ghoti Magazine: "Sustenance"
Poetry Salzburg Review: "Choke-hold"
The Journal (U.K.): "Poetry Class, Room 402,"
    "Family portrait"
Poetry Monthly: "Light happens"
Current Accounts: "Momentum
Great Kills Review: "Poorly lit," "Alms"
FRiGG Magazine: "The made bed," "Chaos theory,"
    "Animus," "Fractured," "Drought," "Almost stung"

811.6
TRI

ISBN 13: 978-1-59948-156-2

Produced in the United States of America

Main Street Rag
PO Box 690100
Charlotte, NC 28227
www.MainStreetRag.com

For mom, who walked with me

Contents

Choke-hold 7

Physical memory 8

Almost stung 9

Fractured 10

Chaos theory 11

Plagiarism 13

Poetry Class, Room 402 14

Family portrait 15

Distance 16

Think of it this way: 17

Process, she asks 18

Sustenance 19

Anchors . .. .20

Drought 21

Harbor . .. .22

Penelope 23

Early thaw . .. .24

Animus . .. .25

Breathless . .. .26

The made bed . .. .27

Of many 28

Alms 29

Once removed . .. .30

Withheld 31

Best laid plans . .. .33

Momentum . .. .34

Residue . .. .35

Coordinates . .. .37

Poorly lit 38

Light happens 40

Choke-hold

but winter:
howling,
chill-choked;
knife-blue sky sharpening
its edge against
the iron of the earth.
Every day an accusation,
even the trees:
branches like bones
pointing,
pewter shards of ice.
It's a lot of

work, this breathing
and breathing:
wind-wheezed;
eyes seamed against
the steel; red hands
weeping white. Air is

less than air. Even
the cypresses
gasping,
drained of color; more
black than green.

Physical memory

This must have been the way
I waited in the womb:
knees up, arms crossed
at the wrists, right hand balled
within the socket of the left.
It's where my body goes when I

forget to pay attention.
For instance: the birdfeeder
off the breakfast room was filled
with suet—that I remember—
and the hornets in the tool shed,
singing of death. Only

once did I stop for gas,
in all those hours and hours,
but by the time I made it home
it was too late; the thing was
done. In retrospect, our voices
were like shards of glass,

murderous—
mesmerizing—

my arms were pleated
tightly to my chest like
the wings of a bat.

Kim Triedman

Almost stung

In the tool shed, shucking peas.

A hornets' nest
between the walls, just above
where her shoulder grazes the rafter.
She is 12; she knows. She can

feel them moving—
the steady whine of them
in her teeth. They haven't

found her yet, but the sun
is hot and she knows they are
coming. Beneath

her arms: the shameful
seep of perspiration. Hands pale
still, and small. The peas

slip silently between her
fingers like beads

of a rosary. Head
dropped, as if

in prayer.

Fractured

Darling

You will

Never know. On my way to work the

Plane fell from the sky, but just a
Small one. The radio played a song
You've never heard before and
My jaw was clamped so tight I couldn't speak.
Everyone thought I was
Crazy or just putting on airs; the sheer
Humiliation. They said I'd
Never truly loved the color green. There were no
Geese up there, either, they must have
Sensed that this was not the best of years
For birds.
When I wake these days my sheets are
Soaked, the water pools between my breasts.
You sleep like you have
Always slept, one foot thrown off the
Far end of the bed.

Chaos Theory

Come this way.
The tree out my window is bare now
then full of leaves; many things, actually, and
the sky likewise changes. Just now there is the
threat of white.

Sometimes: no birds.

I have been here—forever, really—
watching, waiting with a thirst. It may
not seem like much but you will see:
the stories are like the light, so
when I crane my neck a little to the left
the sun is either bleeding or it's not.
Today the road is veined with salt,
but once a moon stared back at me,
blank and unforgiving.

Sometimes there are tears, but there are
copper pennies, too, and glasses of milk;
mothers with no teeth. Paths
abound: citrine, the smell of limes;
kudzu dark and pulpy and heavy as loss.
I have seen a Muslim woman walking
in the wind, her burkha like a flying shroud,
and then the sky above her head
go black with beating birds.

Come this way. I will try to protect you.
I have watched men starve along the way,
half lost, and then devour themselves
like serpents. You will see.
The light this way may be too harsh;
the noise of endless wars. Colors—
mutinous. There are no walls, only space
and then more space—
timeless;
perpetual.

Even on a bad day I will feel you
breathe. It may be quiet. It may be
quiet; only limes.

Come this way.

Plagiarism

(after Tony Hoagland's "A Color of Sky")

Hey babe.
I have a wonderful poem for you

but it's someone else's.
Something about stains and time
and the color of sky—beauty, of course;
relentless. That

phrase he used—
the very tint of inexperience—
it made me want to
bathe in it or sleep; break silently
at a very unlikely angle. The world is

capable of such things—drowning us
on a whim. There are
winter shadows, thin as wire,
and the sky outside my window is
breathless with blue. Above the chimney:
earnest plugs of smoke.
You are that

stain, of course, the one
I can't get out—

ruinous;
glorious;
immutable.

Poetry Class, Room 402

Starting here, the ground goes soft
and Chinese lanterns dance on their wires,
spilling blood at the feet of good people.
Rules are broken and contracts are broken,
assumptions dropped from mean heights like
melons - the soft fuzzed heads of newborn girls.
All that was, was: days like hedgerows;
nights curled tight inside themselves like rage
sliding snake-like on dry bellies
to this strange unholy place.

Starting here, babies are grown men
and grown men are angry; frozen; gruesome
to behold—like death back-loaded, or the opposite
of womb; and anger starting here is loud and fetid
and full of teeth and what we do with it has
everything to do with the softness of the ground,
the softness,
the lanterns,
the waning of the moon,
the tiny but insistent voice of the color of
flame.

Kim Triedman

Family portrait

Flames could erupt at any minute
down the hall; or
downstairs
in the kitchen
a blade, unsheathed might
flash, silver to blue.
Even in the next room
tears can always spring
unbidden, or
hammock themselves
tightly
like corpses
after the blight.

I wait,
suspended in the center,
quivering,
silk peeling from my loins,
all eight of my legs thrumming
to the music of life's
smallest disasters.

Distance

Winter coming, and there must be a
score, any score, the whole thing ending on
a cold day, a hard day, each utterance
too complicated to dissect.

There was the glass of wine, too; don't forget
that. There was the overhead light. Cruel
to be exact. While all around her locusts swarmed
and insults tumbled out of mouths
too tight to form them.
In the refrigerator, a carcass reigned
as though it had something new to offer.

She could hear his voice, faraway as it was.
Between them: cold macadam and dried leaves,
the years flung out like line. She stood,
naked, at the window smeared with grease.
If she knew what he was saying she
didn't let on.

And later, the sheets, pills sliced on the score.
Nighttime dredged of even
the tamest of dreams.

Kim Triedman

Think of it this way:

Between the past and the future
stands a house. It's tidy
and white, nearly ready

to explode. The terror, you see, the
weight of such a thing:
neither here nor there, like words,

withheld, or the hand
that meant to stroke.
Even in a strong wind leaves

can double-back, and
seagulls hang, frozen in sky.
We sit,

burning in silence:
eyes forward—
remembering nothing.

Process, she asks.

I think about
a thousand little weddings,
nightshade and lip gloss,
mealy-mouthed insincerity,
words lilting or hissing or
copulating like cats. All those
rash unholy marriages—
this shadow and that shoulder,
shrunken,
hours or ages ago. Color it
amber. Throw in a
lover, sinewy and fine, or
just the creeping maceration of everyday,
good-enough. Kill the calf,
drip milk into my father's eyes,
but turn off that light, someone, *please.*
It makes me want to spit
into the sink.

Kim Triedman

Sustenance

The evening of the day he died
I ate eggs. I didn't have to

do that—there was food
on every counter. But

standing there one moment
I just noticed I was

making eggs,
moving them around slowly

in the pan, coaxing them
gently·

from one side to
the other. It's the way I

drove home, too—
blunt; suspended; surprised

to be driving. Later,
I remember thinking that

the house felt like
a wayward womb:

swollen, congested,
purpled with dying;

that something
needed to be broken—

to be spilled.

Anchors

It's all about the uterus,
anyway. Everything—
the dance, the deed, that
rip in your favorite stockings.
It all comes round
to the same place
eventually—
brown rooted things and
marl, buds like new nipples;
the twining of vetch. Give me
something to go by—ropey
and rich—give me

menstrual blood.
There is a
kind of peace.

I am waiting for something.

Kim Triedman

Drought

The crows, they
circle, dragging their
wretched shadows, and
light tiptoes
gingerly
as day trips into moon
and fields sprawl
in both directions,
bleached; fallow;
studded with want.
Look here,

I am the thirst;
I am the stubble in the field.
Lull me,
I am wanting.
Sink your fingers deep
and fondle my seed.

Coax me.
Wet me.
Color me wheat.

Harbor

Imagine it:
the wind a ruthless thing,
feral.
Branches shredding
a paper-white sky.

Imagine the house,
imagine the light
in the window—honeyed;
pulpy; weeping like
a womb.

I am there, if you like:
I am the woman in the
broth. Stir me,
I will feel it. Take me to your
mouth. Imagine me
over and over again:

suet, camphor, balm.

Kim Triedman

Penelope

Something like ice;
sky the color of
moon.

It was your voice:
halting,
indistinct.
The absence of story;
absence the story.

Waiting for snow; air
thick with the coming of snow. Sky
turgid,
sallow,
color of moon.

Lies, I know; half-
truths. Sins
of omission.
You needn't have
called.

Blinding, now, brittle
with cold; eyes
bleed and bleed and
sky the color of moon.

Early thaw

The geese were flying west today; it was the

last straw.
Crocuses penetrating; underwear off
before noontime; breath held
thin and high above the collarbone.
I should have guessed:
the groping and the mouthing—
            endlessly—
the dampness of the earth. It was

something:
important,
            immutable—
life asserting itself, insistent
as tongue. Bosoms, hips, the stark
white canvas of throat.
You called. *You*

called. Outside the window:
puddles of snowmelt;
birdsong; cats splaying
shamelessly in the sun
on the front walk.

Kim Triedman

Animus

Evening,
and the copper-colored leaves
shot through with

lingering sun,
malingering sun, slit-

eyed—thin and feckless.

And what do you think about the sky?

I'd be inclined to agree with
whatever you said, and the leaves
red, too, in a certain kind of light.

You could walk down the street -
just that, arms

dangling
and there'd be no malingering

of sun, no
mineral rust; no birds
falling from the air
in a thousand shades of black.

Only the opening:
singular
consummate
church-blue   sky

snatched

like breath
from body earth.

Breathless

I have counted
the buttons on your shirt
and released them,
every one—
stared silent and stung
as the fields of you
unfold before me.
I have sunk my hands deep
and felt your earth,
held it up to my face
to breathe. I have touched it
with my tongue.

Bury me now.
Fill my throat to choking.
Bespread my body.
Press down on me
like swollen loam:
fecund,
full.

Kim Triedman

The made bed

(after Louise Gluck's "The Burning Heart")

Before you, there was the knowledge—
warm, taut, breath reversed,

imprint preceding hand,
dampness anticipating kiss—

only a shape, back then, a space

between words,
between skin.

Something would come, I knew,
a color perhaps—blood

orange, something like flame.
The bed was waiting,

white sheets clean and
softened with age, pillows
smoothed,
silent,
plumped.

Of many

Meet me in the garden
when you're ready.
I'll be the one with

green velvet ears and
the ruby-stained throat.
I have always been here,

plush and poised, rooted
to this earth; perhaps
you haven't noticed.
But I hear you

everywhere—
circling, oscillating, thrumming
like a fever. Non-

commital.

You will see:
we are many
but few; occasionally

sweet. Except for the wind,

there is a kind
of stillness.

Kim Triedman

Alms

All this I have offered:
three fingers on a cheek. Words like
unguents. The private room.

Bend it: my will—you always have. Twist it
nearly to breaking. Plough it
deep into the dark. I will

allow it,
endlessly,
endlessly accommodate the dance, the

door, the back of your head—lovely
it is. None of this new,
none of this old.

These things I have offered:
three jewels—
two copper coins—
the inside of my throat.

Once removed

your mind a bluish thing, twilit.
I have felt it, many times:
the squint of eyes, abstraction of hands,
the light of late afternoon

laddering its way through
broken clouds; even the cormorants,
blacker than oil, hanging their wings
out to dry. The way you

follow a thought like a tune,
half-listening-half-dreaming, in and out
of time, plumbing its bluish depths.
Never mind: I am not meant

to understand. The rocks are
black, the seaweed roils like
tangled dreadlocks in the foam;
the tonguing of the waves. Your face

a blank.

Kim Triedman

Withheld

Don't make things so

complicated. It's only
plonk we're drinking, and
the napkins, paper. The

baby, well, she'll need a bath, but
later, when the doves purl

and the sky begins to
run like milk. That was

you, toothless

once,
simple in your time.

I can picture the fists

balled, the rivered snot;
I can picture the
rapture of your

squint-eyed fury.
So clean it was; so clean it was

then:
pure and mocking as
a primary color—

something that would burn
if you held it too close
or looked at it straight on,

like the sun.

Kim Triedman

Best laid plans

This is how it works:

You are there—
The slap, the squall. You make the
Breakfasts, such as they are, the
Beds; feel the foreheads with your lips.

This, too, is how it works:

Winter boots. Suns, up and down. They cry or they
Laugh; eventually, they grow
Breasts.

Sometimes, a difficult night.

This is how it works:

You stay put.
The years slide beneath your feet.

This is how it's supposed to work:

You are here, they are there, them with their breasts, their
Apartments. You still with your
Lips. They are breathless; there will be
Thanksgivings and
Futures. Their tears, when they come, are pressed
Flat against their palms.

This is how it works:

You—
Still with your lips.

Momentum

On the fifth day of the snow
the daughter leaves, saying,
I may be back.
The sky does not exist.
In the kitchen: soup, simmering
until the end of time.

The mother.
It is the long hour before dinner, and
dark. She walks,
from the kitchen to the hallway
and turns, looks back
to the beginning.

On the fifth day of the snow
the daughter leaves, saying
I have no choice.
The sky exists, but it is elsewhere
and oh so many colors. There is
a pulse, like drums, there is the
suck of red.

No, she says, gathering her
things about her, *I don't care
for any soup.*

Kim Triedman

Residue

Yesterday there was too much
room in the world. Eyes; breath;
the willow weeping, and
always the damage—
words swallowed whole,
tremors at fault lines;
the sharp mean memory of sun,
leaves gone. Still,
occasionally, I find her
ballet tights in the laundry.
I fold them slowly,
set them on the stair up to her room.
On the phone she sounds
quite breathless: a paper's due;
the Kirov's coming to New York
next month. She speaks so fast
I only listen to the speed.

It's obvious now:
time rushing through and standing still;
the sky, aubergine.
None of it planned—
not the wind circling like hawks,
not the blight. It's dark at four,
her shins are tired; I wonder is it
late enough to pour a glass of wine.
The house fills up with too much space,
each cat now has a room
to call her own.
I used to love my bedroom door, but now
I leave it open.

Between breaths, the only lasting solace
the table; the lamp; the thick round
custard of light.

Kim Triedman

Coordinates

The father dies.
This is the beginning.

Start again.
The son.
Across the room a nurse sits down
to stroke the father's hand. Still
warm, purpled with dying but
pliant, too; responsive as thirst. She dips
a cloth. Brings some water to his lips.

Across the room: the son, watching.
How small, a man—
the root; the quotient that remains.
What does he measure now?
Where does his shadow end?

the son wonders, holding his
own hands.

Quadrants shift, conflate.
Nothing is fixed:
the body—
the walls—
the point   of intersection.

Poorly lit

When I was a kid maybe
8 or 10

or 15 I used to think
that life was pretty perfect,
my life, that is,
the loving parents,
good hair,

etc. but what I
really couldn't understand
at the time
was the way
Sunday evenings
made me want
to die:
the quiet the quiet
the overhead lights in every
room of the house
too dim or
too bright and
my mother upstairs
napping
far away under
her favorite afghan.
I should have known then
what I

Kim Triedman

know now, that
that is where my
future was forming,
not in the straight A's
straight teeth not in
the good graces
god or anyone else
had thought to bestow
but in the belly
of those long, poorly-
lit Sunday evenings, under

the nasty blue glow
of a TV
that nobody
was watching.

Light happens

It began by snowing, first,
before waking, just
a thin spittle nearly a rain

grayer than white.
Contemptible. So
thin, really, so

ruined: the sky bullying,
the ground wet with it and mean,
just that.

By ten it amounted, like lint:
pinches and pockets
all along the north side

and weary, too. Winds slipped,
fell; decades of hours
then noontime erupted

in a bedlam of blue.
Treetops—blackened,
bejeweled—ancient

as hands, trembling:
death-crook'd fingers against
a perfect newborn sky.

Kim Triedman

With Gratitude

These, from the depths:

To my family, in all its incarnations:

    the immediate—Eric, eternally, for creating the room; Hanna,
        Charlotte, and Sophie, for stepping into it
    the original —Mom and Dad, John, Scott, and Julie, all beloved
    the amended —Nancy (also beloved)
    the appended—John Oldsman, much missed, and Gloria,
        much adored
    and the extended—Grandma, for all that is soft in me, and the
        whole gang, east and west coast

I'd like to thank Paul and Matthew, biblical both.

I'd also like to thank the following, without whom this book would never have become: The Poetry Group, always fluid but certainly including Joanne, Laura, Ariadne, Lorian, Diane, Sara, Betsy, and Ann; my comrades from Colrain; Nadia Herman Colburn, for just about everything; Chris Smither, for the soundtrack; and Micah, for the beautiful cover.

Special thanks to Jeffrey Levine and Joan Houlihan, who gave more in three days than any other could have managed in three years.

And a quiet one to the little ivory muse that's perched in my heart.